30 THINGS
I TELL MYSELF AND OTHERS

Volume One

IKE ISINGUZO

Unless otherwise indicated, all Scripture quotations are taken from the *Holy Bible, New International Version*®. NIV®. Copyright © 1973, 1978, 1984 by International Bible Society. Used by permission of Zondervan Publishing House. All Rights Reserved.

Scripture quotations marked NKJV are taken from the *New King James Version*. Copyright © 1979, 1980, 1982, Thomas Nelson, Inc.

Scripture quotations marked KJV are taken from the *Holy Bible, King James Version*.

30 Things I Tell Myself and Others
ISBN: 0-88144-299-2
Copyright © 2008 by Ike Isinguzo

Printed by
Victory Graphics and Media
9731 East 54th Street
Tulsa, Oklahoma 74146
www.victorygraphicsandmedia.com

Printed in the United States of America. All rights reserved under International Copyright Law. Contents and/or cover may not be reproduced in whole or in part in any form without the express written consent of the Author.

DEDICATION

This book is dedicated to the Holy Spirit of God Almighty, who has made something out of nothing and somebody out of nobody!

TABLE OF CONTENTS

1	Put God First	7
2	Seek God's Opinion, Not Man's	9
3	Pray and See God's Favor	14
4	Laugh Your Troubles Away	18
5	Speak Your Desires	20
6	Give God the Glory	25
7	Yield to the Spirit	28
8	Let Your Faith Be Productive	33
9	God Will Never Abandon You	35
10	Hold On to Your Promise	37
11	Know When to Move Up	40
12	Acquire Knowledge and Excel	43
13	Let God Make You What You Ought to Be	45
14	Sow Seeds of Unconditional Love	47
15	Release God's Greatness in You	49
16	Make Your Move and Trust God to Perfect It	51
17	Team Up With a Faithful God	53
18	Purity Releases Power	55
19	Trust God with Your Heart	58
20	Be Diligent in Your Work	61
21	Don't Let Your Past Dictate Your Future	64
22	Forgiveness: The Secret to An Open Heaven	67
23	Read to Lead	70

24	Listen to God	72
25	A New Heart for a New Glory	74
26	Believe and See	77
27	Take the High Road in Jesus	79
28	Don't Procrastinate	82
29	Let God Teach You	84
30	Don't Repeat Your Failures	89
Acknowledgements		93
About the Author		95

Put God First

"IN THE BEGINNING GOD…" [Gen. 1:1]

Everything begins with God. Therefore, when you give God first place in your life, heaven goes out of its way to reward your humility with greatness and God will give you your own new beginning! In the Book of Genesis, Joseph refused to defile himself with Potiphar's wife because he did not want to do any wicked thing against God (**"How then could I do such a wicked thing and sin against God?"**—Genesis 39:9) or against man. The world will see Jesus and the fruit of His Spirit in us when we make God the top priority of all we say and do. Then God's favor will be evident and His glory revealed in our lives.

His glory manifested in our lives will make life enjoyable and satisfactory! Remember, if God is not in what you are doing, then no matter how hard you try, it will not happen. For example, no matter how much the prophets of Baal shouted [1 King 18], no fire came down from heaven for them. But when the prophet Elijah, a man who knew the secret of putting God first, called upon God, fire came down from heaven, consumed the sacrifice and licked up the water. Here is Elijah's prayer:

"O LORD, answer me, so these people will know that you, O LORD, are God, and that you are turning their hearts back again." [1 Kings 18:;37]

And, as a result of Elijah's prayer, this is what happened:

"Then the fire of the LORD fell and burned up the sacrifice, the wood, the stones and the soil, and also licked up the water in the trench. When all the people saw this, they fell prostrate and cried, 'The LORD he is God! The LORD he is God!" [1 Kings 18:38-39].

Elijah's heartbeat was that God's people would know the only true God and that their hearts would be turned back to Him. God is looking for men like Elijah who will know Him intimately and who will love Him more than they love themselves! Elijah was not there to prove that he was a powerful prophet or heavily anointed or to be reverenced. No, he was there to point them back to relationship with God:

"...so these people will know that you, O LORD, are God, and that you are turning their hearts back again." [1 Kings 18:37]

As a result of Elijah's prayer, Israel was changed forever! Beloved, when you align your vision with God's vision, God Himself will back you up with signs and wonders. Take this truth to your heart: The kingdom of God is not about your agenda, but God's. In Matthew 6:33 we see Jesus saying this very thing:

"But seek first His kingdom and his righteousness, and all these things will be given to you as well."

To impact this generation for Christ, please do not run after *all these things*. Rather run after God; "chase" Him and seek His kingdom. When you make Him your priority, He will do the same for you and *all these things* will run after you!

2
Seek God's Opinion, Not Man's

POPULARITY DOES NOT DETERMINE productivity and fame is no guarantee of destiny! Rather, it is your energy and creativity, mixed with reverence for God that supercharges your productivity. A higher level of productivity opens the door for promotion. Therefore, trying to be promoted without productivity is like trying to harvest before cultivation! In a letter to the church in Ephesus, the Apostle Paul writes:

"…We are not trying to please men but God, who tests our hearts" [1 Thessalonians 2:4].

"Slaves, obey your earthly masters with respect and fear, and with sincerity of heart, just as you would obey Christ. Obey them not only to win their favor when their eye is on you, but like slaves of Christ, doing the will of God from your heart. Serve wholeheartedly, as if you were serving the LORD, not men, because you know that the LORD will reward everyone for whatever good he does, whether he is slave or free." [Ephesians 6:5-8].

Working with the aim of pleasing man rather than God amounts to working towards frustration. Why? Because you will never be able to fully satisfy man. That is why it is important that we understand that we are called to:

"…Find out what pleases the Lord." [Eph. 5:10].

Clarify for yourself what pleases the Lord, by seeking Him and His kingdom. When you do this and give yourself wholly to it, it will put you on the path of destiny and the roadmap to greatness. Let your aim be to impress God and touch His heart, by finding out what He desires. When you touch His heart, He will touch the heart of men for you! What more will He do? He will also use you to touch the heart of nations. King David was an excellent example of this. Because David was a man after God's heart, God did not hesitate to enthrone him and to dethrone Saul, a man whose only aim was to impress people. Listen to what the prophet Samuel told Saul:

"You acted foolishly…. You have not kept the command the Lord your God gave you; if you had, He would have established your kingdom over Israel for all time. But now your kingdom will not endure; the Lord has sought out *a man after His own heart* and appointed him leader of his people, because you have not kept the Lord's command." [1 Samuel 13:13-14, emphasis mine].

What had Saul done to prompt this response in God?

"Saul remained at Gilgal, and all the troops with him were quaking with fear. He waited seven days, the time set by Samuel; but Samuel did not come to Gilgal, and Saul's men began to scatter. So, he said, 'Bring me the burnt offering and the fellowship offerings.' And Saul offered up the burnt offering. Just as he finished making the offering, Samuel arrived, and Saul went out to greet him.

"What have you done?" asked Samuel. Saul replied, *'When I saw that the men were scattering,* and that you did not come at the set time, and that the Philistines were assembling at Michmash, I thought, 'Now the Philistines will come down against me at Gilgal, and I have not sought the LORD's favor.' *So I felt compelled* to offer the burnt offering.'" [1 Samuel 13:7-12, emphasis mine].

How God felt was simply not important to Saul. All he wanted to do was impress the people, which is evident in this verse, "...*When I saw... the men ... scattering...I felt compelled...*" People always act foolishly when all they think about is how to impress men. You cannot be God's "man" when you are the people's "man." You are either one or the other. If Saul had focused on God, and had been more concerned about the honor of God, his kingdom would have enjoyed eternal glory like David's. Friend, God is much more interested in where our hearts are focused and not as much on what our bodies are doing, or what our mouths seem to be saying. God is more concerned with our hearts than our outward appearances. As He Himself says:

"The LORD does not look at the things man looks at. Man looks at the outward appearance, but the LORD looks at the heart." [1 Samuel 16:7].

"For as he thinks in his heart, so he is." [Proverbs 23:7 NKJV]

Who you are is clearly known to God by the focus of your heart. Whereas Saul made decisions without God, David did not make them himself, even when faced with more seemingly hopeless situations than Saul. Rather, David sought God's face and heart before doing anything. He was a man after God's own heart. On one occasion, after returning to their homes on a certain day, David and his men discovered that their homes were not only burnt and destroyed, but also that their wives and children had been taken away by their enemies.

"So David and his men wept aloud until they had no strength left to weep."

What else?

"David was greatly distressed because the *men were talking of stoning him;* each one was bitter in spirit because of his sons and daughters. But David found strength in the LORD his God." [1 Samuel 30:4, 6, emphasis mine].

How did God deliver David from this distressing situation? . Let's find out:

"David enquired of the LORD, "Shall I pursue this raiding party? Will I overtake them?" … "Pursue them…. you will certainly overtake them and succeed in the rescue." [1 Samuel 30:8].

These accounts clearly reveal two men with two different hearts: Saul's heart was to impress and appease men while David's heart was totally sold out to God and God's desires. May you be like David was for this generation; May you please God. May God say that He has found in you someone whose heart is after His. May your heart be totally sold out to God, and may you care less about pleasing men. Your godly character will shine and the glory of God will be manifested in your life, when you make God the first priority in your life!

Saul did not respect God nor the things of God. By contrast, David had respect for Abiathar, the priest of the LORD [see 1 Samuel 30:7].

"Be imitators of God, therefore…and live a life of love, just as Christ loved us and gave himself up for us as a fragrant offering and sacrifice to God." [Eph. 5:1].

You please God by imitating Christ. Imitating Christ is an enviable addiction and indication that God has become your delight. When He becomes all you ever desire, rest is guaranteed. As the Psalmist said:

"Delight yourself in the Lord and he will give you the desires of your heart." [Psalm 37:4].

When God is your desire, your desires become His! Aiming at God's heart, and indeed, impressing God, divinely connects you to the glorious mindset of Christ which in turn ushers you into your rest:

"For anyone who enters God's rest also rests from his own work, just as God did from his." [Hebrews 4:10].

3

Prayer Brings Favor

"VERY EARLY IN THE morning, while it was still dark, Jesus got up, left the house and went off to a solitary place, where he prayed. Simon and His companions went to look for him, and when they found Him, they exclaimed: 'Everyone is looking for you.'" [Mark 1:35-37].

Heaven compels everyone and everything good to look out for you when you seek God and spend quality time with Him. In other words, the forces of life begin to work in your favor when your attention to the kingdom of God is a matter of top priority and utmost exclusivity in your life. Favor is not natural, but rather it is the supernatural intervention of God and as such, it cannot be maneuvered. Spending time with God stirs up the supernatural on your behalf and establishes your candidacy for divine favor! Jesus never had to go looking for anyone, but as he fellowshipped with the Father and tarried in His presence… God released His angels who brought everyone to Jesus. God's presence is all you need, because He is the Source from whom all blessings come!

We are talking about intensive, effective, fervent prayers that come from the heart. We are not talking about casual, routine, rote kind of prayers.

Rather, we are talking about the kind of prayers that Elijah and Hannah prayed, where everything in you is praying: your heart is being emptied to God; your spiritual eye is totally focused on heaven and you are not distracted by the things of this earth. Jesus gave us an excellent example of this kind of prayer, and that is why His ministry was full of signs and wonders. When He prayed, He was totally focused on the Father.

"And being in anguish, he prayed more earnestly, and His sweat was like drops of blood falling to the ground." [Luke 22:44].

As a result of this kind of prayer, Jesus received the power to triumph on the cross of Calvary. The devil was humiliated and there was nothing he could do to alter Jesus' mission.

Could it be that challenges linger too long for some of God's people because they have wrong attitudes in prayer? Perhaps some of us have treated the things of God too casually. Our God takes the issues pertaining to His children seriously! God does not need our help, He is the Almighty! But if we, who really need God's help come to Him without any sense of urgency or emergency, our case might be treated as such! For example, the medical attention given to a patient brought into the Emergency Room [ER] of a hospital by an ambulance would be much more swift than for a person who felt a slight headache and decided to walk into a clinic. You do not need a doctor's appointment to visit a walk-in clinic, you just need to wait your turn. In that case, the doctor owes you no apology if you have to wait for quite a while to see him because the situation is not serious. In like manner, men that have impacted history and indeed their generations for God, have been men of immense passion and commitment to their callings. There was nothing casual about their prayers, but rather they were passionate and unreserved. You can readily understand that from Isaiah's zeal. Let's read his prayer:

"For Zion's sake I will not keep silent, for Jerusalem's sake I will not remain quiet, till her righteousness shines out like the dawn, her salvation like a blazing torch." [Isaiah 62:1]

With God's help you can terminate your singleness, poverty, sickness, stagnation, frustration, confusion, depression and indeed, all manner of setbacks in your life. Adopt Isaiah's attitude and take those situations to God with effective, earnest and fervent prayers.

Do you remember Jabez? He was frustrated, devastated and utterly tormented by a demonic force that was working against his destiny. But Jabez didn't take the situation lightly; rather he took it seriously and prayed accordingly. His prayers were delivered to God at an emergency speed and heaven responded instantly. His destiny was restored on a glorious scale!

Hannah is another example of taking prayer seriously. She would have died a barren woman and Peninnah would have had the last laugh if Hannah had not risen up and prayed her heart out to God:

"In bitterness of soul Hannah wept much and prayed to the LORD.... As she kept praying to the LORD, Eli observed her mouth. Hannah was praying in her heart, and her lips were moving but her voice was not heard." [1 Samuel 1:10, 12].

Even if you have been experiencing some rocky moments in your marriage, you can experience romance again through the power of prayer. With God's power working in and through you, there is nothing you and He can't accomplish together. You can have wholeness in your relationships, be a success both in work and ministry and accomplish things you never even dreamed of! Friend, there is nothing impossible for you if only you will begin to pray more earnestly, more "aggressively", more intensively, more effectively and more deeply!

Say goodbye to ineffectual, surfacy, lip-oriented prayers. Your prayer life can be so energized that there's no time for distractions. Deep-rooted, heartfelt prayers will always bring down the finger of the Most High God. Pharaoh and his magicians saw that finger and dared not keep the Israelites in Egypt a day longer. In the same way, no weapon formed against you will prosper. As you begin to provoke heaven with intensified prayers, all opposition in your life will begin to crumble. As you engage heaven in meaningful petition, things that have not been working for you will begin to function. Just as Hezekiah turned his face to the wall and obtained instant healing and longevity, as you hold firmly onto the feet of God in prayer, everything that may have brought you shame, sickness or death will be eternally obliterated from your life. Beloved, arise and pray! Take your prayers seriously and God will take your destiny seriously!

4
Laugh Your Troubles Away

LAUGH AT YOUR TROUBLES and they will succumb to your laughter.

"They called the apostles in and had them *flogged*. Then they ordered them not to speak in the name of Jesus, and let them go. The apostles left the Sanhedrin, *rejoicing* because they had been counted worthy of suffering disgrace for the Name." [Acts 5:40-41, emphasis mine].

It wouldn't make sense in the natural to see an elderly person rejoice after they had been assaulted. But that is exactly what the apostles did in the face of opposition and persecution from the devil. It only served to increase their zeal for God, and as a result, the Lord was pleased and He released more grace to them for evangelism:

"Day after day, in the temple courts and from house to house, they never stopped teaching and proclaiming the good news that Jesus is the Christ." [Acts 5: 42].

Troubles and persecutions could not stop the apostles or the Gospel. Our troubles are not meant to stop or discourage us but are "designed" to

Laugh Your Troubles Away

provoke the divine power within us. Indeed, all our troubles have already been overcome by the Lord, which is why the devil attempts to make things that really are blessings look as though they are troubles. Jesus said:

"In this world you will have trouble. But take heart! I have overcome the world." [John 16:33].

If there were any unconquered trouble still threatening us the Lord would have told us., But there is none because Jesus said; **"It is finished."** [John 19:30]. Your ability to maintain and sustain your joy in the face of adversity is a significant indication that you are growing spiritually. Our growth is doubtful when we complain and cry at every whim of trial, and when we run from church to church seeking miracles. There is no challenge that can come your way that is capable of drowning you. God will not permit you to experience any trial that is beyond your control. Laughing and rejoicing annoys the enemy. Why? Because he doesn't want to see you happy, he desires to see you in sorrow and pain....It makes his day when you are frustrated, stressed out, confused, intimidated, and depressed. The enemy does not want you to be happy, to be joyful and to rejoice. So, when you laugh, rejoice, dance, and celebrate; when you are jubilant and testify to the goodness of the Lord, you destroy the devil. The enemy cannot stand that. You wear him out; you torment him. He's shattered emotionally and spiritually when you celebrate! Why? Because your rejoicing attracts God into your battles! When God appears, the battle is won! He takes over from you and humiliates the devil and his works against your life!

Let God do the fighting for you today! Celebrate, be jubilant, dance, rejoice, praise God and worship Him in the beauty of His holiness! That is all you need for that wall of frustration and trouble to fall!

5

Speak Your Desires

"…IF ANYONE SAYS TO this mountain, 'Go throw yourself into the sea,' and does not doubt in his heart but believes that what he says will happen, it will be done for him." [Mark 11: 22].

The "mountains" that people experience in life are the ones they either hesitate or refuse to command out of their lives, or they are the troubles that they think they cannot command out of their destinies. Friend, please recognize that you have been authorized to uproot and to plant, to bind and to loose, as it is written:

"See, today I appoint you over nations and kingdoms to uproot and tear down, to destroy and overthrow, to build and to plant." [Jeremiah 1:10];

"Every plant that my heavenly Father has not planted will be pulled up by roots." [Matthew 15:13],

"Whatever you bind on earth will be bound in heaven, and whatever you loose on earth will be loosed in heaven." [Matthew 18:18] and;

"And every tongue which rises against you in judgment you shall condemn. This is the heritage of the servants of the LORD." [Isaiah 54:17 NKJV].

Your destiny corresponds with your declarations, and they will determine your celebrations! What you cannot declare you cannot take delivery of! For if you *shall say it*…then you *will have it!* When you say *it* and believe *it*, then *it* will happen, but if you do not say *it*, *it* will not be done. It will equally not happen if you only say *it* and do not believe *it*. That is the implication of what our sweet Jesus said in Mark 11:12. Please meditate on this Scripture:

"**The tongue has the power of life and death, and those who love it will eat its fruit.**" [Proverbs 18:21].

You can give *life* to your life and destiny by the power that is in your tongue. Equally, you can destroy whatever you don't like in your life with your tongue. Jesus said: "**The words I have spoken to you are spirit and they are life.** [John 6:63] Why? Because, as He said:

"**For just as the Father raises the dead and gives them life, even so the Son gives life to whom he is pleased to give it.**" [John 5:21].

Again Jesus says:

"**As the Father has sent me, I am sending you.**" [John 20:21].

In other words, you are adequately entitled and empowered to operate in the class of Jesus and the Father. Your words can give life or death because you are in Jesus and Jesus is in you and Jesus is in the Father [John 14:20]. Again, as Jesus is in heaven so are we now [1 John 4:17]. Do not watch your marriage, education, business, spiritual life, relationships, children or spouse "die"; pronounce life unto them! In like manner, pronounce death to whatever you don't desire and it will wither. Jesus demonstrated this power in Mark 11:12-25 when He cursed the fig tree. Peter marveled at the speed at which the tree withered and died within 24 hours of Jesus cursing it! Peter said:

"Rabbi, look! The fig tree you cursed has withered!" [Mark 11:21].

Poverty, sickness, disease, failure, stagnation, frustration, disappointment, fear, anxiety, debt, doubt, rejection, dejection, depression, oppression, anger, malice and all manner of satanic oppressions will exit your life now if you will open your mouth and pronounce a curse upon them! Bind the devil from working in your life! Declare yourself free from his devices. Speak your destiny in Jesus. Curse the poverty in your life; declare your prosperity. See life coming back to your family and your business! Friend, you can do whatever Jesus did and even more if you believe and have faith in Him. As Jesus Himself said:

"I tell you truth, anyone who has faith in me will do what I have been doing. He will do even greater things than these, because I am going to the Father. And I will do whatever you ask in my name, so that the Son may bring glory to the Father. You may ask for anything in my name, and I will do it." [John 14:12-14].

Your destiny will blossom by the spiritual fertilizer of your words. Your abundance is awaiting your pronouncements. What you'll see in your tomorrow will be the harvest of words that you sow today!. Why? Because:

"From the fruit of his mouth a man's stomach is filled; with the harvest from his lips he is satisfied." [Proverbs 18:20]

From the words of his mouth a man's life is filled with his possessions; from the words of his mouth a man realizes his dreams; and from the words of his mouth a man begins to celebrate the favor of God upon his life! It is important to note that one fruit cannot be described as a harvest.

Rather a harvest is an abundance of fruits. The word says: "…**With the harvest from his lips he is satisfied.**" [Proverbs 18:20] When you continue to speak to the barren places in your life, to your adversities, to your stagnation, to your frustration and to any situation you despise, you succeed in wearing them out. Do you remember the wicked judge in Luke 18:1-8 who neither feared God nor cared about man? Jesus said that judge could not withstand the persistent widow who came to him everyday for justice. The judge finally had to admit:

"Even though I don't fear God or care about men, yet because this widow keeps bothering me, I will see that she gets justice, so that she won't eventually wear me out with her coming." [Luke 18:4]

Friend, that wicked judge is the devil and his demons! Don't be afraid to bother them terribly! Why? Because if you refuse to bother them they will bother you instead! Don't keep your mouth shut; wear the devil out, trouble your troublers until they are worn out and die. Don't be gentle with the devil, he is not nice. He is a thief, a killer and a destroyer! *Steal* his peace before he steals yours; *kill* him before he kills you and *destroy* him before he destroys you! How do you do all that? Use your tongue! Why? Because: **"The tongue has the power of life and death, and those who love it will eat its fruit."** [Proverbs 18:21] What your tongue speaks life to is what will have life in your destiny, and what your tongue pronounces dead is dead already!

As stated earlier, keep saying whatever you desire until it rains! Why? Because: **"If clouds are full of water, they pour rain upon the earth."** [Ecclesiastes 11:3]. Keep saying what you desire until the spiritual cloud is so saturated with your words that it cannot hold on to them any longer. It will be forced to give them up as rain in obedience to the divine laws of God! Friend, don't worry about how long you must keep speaking! Please keep speaking until there are victorious events and glorious effects; keep saying it…a day…a week…a month…a year; even a decade until you see it happen! Don't give up! Remember, the devil's #1 aim is to see you give up so that he can crush you, but please don't. Keep saying what you desire until you frustrate him and he flees! The devil was created not to withstand you; but to be afraid of you!

Now that you know these secrets, it is time to stop suffering and start prospering! Use your tongue to speak words of life and things will fall into place for you!

6
Give God the Glory

"ON THE APPOINTED DAY Herod, wearing his royal robes, sat on his throne and delivered a public address to the people. They shouted, 'This is the voice of a god, not of man.' Immediately, because Herod did not give praise to God, an angel of the LORD struck him down, and he was eaten by worms and died." [Acts 12:21-23].

Herod did not actually need anyone to praise him for doing right. After all, he was already a king. He was royalty; he already sat on a throne, and was already ruling. So, he actually didn't need anyone to send him to hell ahead of time. That said, his pride, arrogance and selfishness catalyzed his peril. Friend, you are already a king, and a prince of the Most High [1 Peter 2:9], of and from heaven like Jesus Christ the Prince of Peace, God in His unfathomable love and wisdom has made us co-heirs with Jesus [Galatians 3:26-29].

By your redemption, you became a son of God and a heavenly citizen [1 Corinthians 15:48]. You are already glorified, beautified and enthroned [Ephesians 2:6]. So you really don't need anyone to flatter you and corrupt your sanctity with pride. You are already made, as the word says; **"Praise** be to the God and Father of our LORD Jesus Christ, who has blessed us in heavenly realms with every spiritual blessing in Christ." [Ephesians 1:3]. So, you are not here on earth to show off, rather you are here to showcase God's glory. The ultimate showdown will be with the devil, to bring down the pride of the kingdom of darkness. Scripture reveals this to us:

"[God's] intent was that now, through the church, the manifold wisdom of God should be made known to the rulers and authorities in the heavenly realms, according to His eternal purpose which he accomplished in Christ Jesus our LORD." [Ephesians 3:10].

You are here for business, serious kingdom business as an ambassador of Christ! Anyone on a diplomatic mission has been sent as an ambassador; his mission is to accomplish the will of his king and the purposes of his kingdom. Jesus is our King and heaven is our kingdom; our goal is to satisfy Him and bring joy to His heart. Thus, we are not concerned with the applause and encouragement of men. As the Apostle Paul said: "I know whom I have believed, and am convinced that he is able to guard what I have entrusted to him for that day." [2 Timothy 1:12]. We know whom we have believed in (Jesus) and our reward comes from Him.

However, it is not evil to take compliments. Do not be afraid to take well-intended and genuine compliments from people who truly appreciate your accomplishments. But it is wise to instantly acknowledge the Source of all blessings and refute all flattery that is intended to breed pride, arrogance and death! Compliments from a pure heart are spices that work wonders in our lives. Learn to discern through the Holy Spirit, the difference between pure compliments and flattering words. And always remember to give God praise for whatever mighty works He is doing in your life and ministry.

"With flattery he will corrupt those who have violated the covenant, but the people who know their God will firmly resist him." [Dan 11:32].

Flattery corrupts destinies and perverts justice. It is a spiritual seduction that lures many into dungeons of destruction. Please note that corruption from flattery is targeted against those who violate the covenant. Who are they? They are those who do not have the fear of God in them and who do not obey the word of God. The flattery of the devil runs over where the fear of God is lacking. Do you know why? I'll tell you: if you do not obey God and His word, there is only one other person you must obey: the devil! If you don't want to obey the devil and be corrupted by his flattery, then obey God and His word and you'd be glorified by His blessings! **"What do we have that we did not receive from Him?"** Please remember that everything we have is from Him! Again, it is wisdom to acknowledge that: **"Every good and perfect gift is from above, coming down from the Father of the heavenly lights, who does not change like shifting shadows."** [James 1:17]. Therefore, acknowledge the Giver; give Him glory, honor, praise and worship. Appreciate the gifts He has given you, and put them into effective efficient use for His kingdom purposes!

Yield to the Spirit

"ALL THIS I HAVE spoken while still with you. But the Counselor, the Holy Spirit whom the Father will send in My name, will teach you all things and will remind you of everything I have said to you." [John 14:25-26].

The Holy Spirit will remind and teach you all things, so that you are able to understand the deep mysteries of God. As a result, your life will become empty of struggles, regrets and dryness. It's no wonder the Bible says:

"His divine power has given us everything we need for life and godliness through our knowledge of him who called us by his own glory and goodness." [2 Peter 1:3].

When you focus on knowing and walking with the Holy Spirit and letting go of all you are and have, all impossibilities, barriers and weaknesses in your life will be destroyed. As it is written:

"…For My strength is made perfect in weakness." [2 Corinthians 12:9 NKJV].

You will see souls saved, and miracles happen when the Holy Spirit moves through you as you are TOTALLY yielded to Him. The Holy Spirit reveals and glorifies Jesus through vessels who are careless about the world but care much about the things of God. Are you willing to be that vessel? Allow yourself to become overwhelmingly thirsty for the Holy Spirit. Be thirsty enough to receive the rain, which is His anointing. As the scriptures say:

"For I will pour water on the thirsty land, and streams on the dry ground; I will pour my Spirit on your offspring. They will spring up like grass in a meadow, like poplar trees by flowing streams." [Isaiah 44:3-4].

The anointing makes all the difference in your life. The anointing will distinguish you; it will confer on you the spirit of excellence; it will make you stand out from the multitude; it will put an end to your struggling and toil. The anointing is the only guarantee to your all-round success. It will open doors of favor to you and shut doors of destruction. The devil is forced to flee when the anointing shows up because it makes things happen. The speed you need is in the anointing. It guarantees you wisdom, understanding and universal knowledge. It is a shield to those who possess it and it will guide you, promote you, and release clarity of mind. It will connect you to greatness, deliver you from trouble, and give you everything you need ["His divine power [*anointing*] has given us everything we need for life and godliness through our knowledge of him who called us by his own glory and goodness"—[2 Peter 1:3,emphasis mine]. I cannot overemphasize this truth! Simply put, you need the anointing! It is the power of God for all kingdom purposes!

Jesus received the indwelling presence of the Holy Spirit after His baptism in the Jordan by John the Baptist:

"As soon as Jesus was baptized, he went up out of the water. At that moment heaven was opened, and He saw the Spirit of God descending like a dove and lighting on him. And a voice from heaven said, 'This is My Son, whom I love; with Him I am well pleased.'" [Matthew 3:16].

The indwelling presence of the Holy Spirit is the first level of anointing. Jesus received it at the Jordan, but that was not enough for His ministry, He needed not only the indwelling but a "Rain"; a continuous outpour of the Holy Spirit. He needed an immeasurable amount of the Holy Spirit, and He went for it! How, when and where? The scriptures tell us:

"Jesus, full of the Holy Spirit, returned from the Jordan and was led by the Spirit in the desert, where for forty days He was tempted by the devil. He ate nothing during those days, and at the end of them He was hungry." [Luke 4:1-2]

It is important to acknowledge the indwelling presence of the Holy Spirit. His presence is awesome and absolutely amazing! But any child of God that wants to make an impact through his destiny and to his generation needs a higher level of anointing! Not only do you need the indwelling anointing, but also the ongoing rain! You cannot compare the effect of water in a cup (i.e. the indwelling) to that of a downpour of rain! If you spilled the water in a cup, or if you drank it, or the cup got broken, that would be the end of the story! But when the rain falls, it fills not only the cup, but also the lake, the river, and the ocean. The effects of a flood are overwhelming!

The Holy Spirit separated Jesus into the desert so He could receive this overflowing Rain… Jesus needed to be alone with God. A very high level of focus was required so that He could do this. Maximum undivided attention is the key to the Rain! Through that divine separation, the Holy

Spirit removed every anti-anointing distraction. Like Jesus, to receive this Rain, you need to separate yourself unto the Holy Spirit. You need to let go of everything and everyone and go unreservedly for that "oil" of the Spirit that causes everything to run smoothly. Why did Jesus go into the desert? Was it to fast and pray? And what happened as a result of that separation? God, the Father released the anointing, the rain, without measure upon Him! You too can do like Jesus did and your story will change for the best! As it says in the word:

"Jesus returned [*from the desert*] to Galilee in the power of the Spirit, and news about Him spread through the whole countryside." [Luke 4:14, emphasis mine]

Why would news about Him spread through the whole area even before He opened His mouth to say anything? The answer is found in Acts 10:38:

"God anointed Jesus of Nazareth with the Holy Spirit and power, and…he went around doing good and healing all who were under the power of the devil, because God was with Him."

It is the anointing of God upon you that will announce you; not your oratory skills or important associations [according to Dr. Paul Enenche; people may associate with highly anointed vessels and still not be connected to the grace of God upon their lives (e.g. Judas Iscariot sat and ate with Jesus, yet Judas died with no anointing!)] Your heart is much more important in receiving the rain than your mouth!

Dr Paul Enenche said: *"Anointing is the outcome of God's presence."* In other words, the anointing reveals the powerful presence of Almighty God on a vessel or in a place! It went ahead of Jesus and began to alert the whole area about Him. That same anointing upon Jesus is still speaking for Him today and is still working wonders all over the world: the blind see, the lame walk, the dead are raised, and demons are being cast out at the mention of His name!

If you are hungry enough for the anointing, it can also be transmitted to you through the laying on of hands. As Paul said to Timothy:

"Do not neglect your gift [*anointing*], which was given you through a prophetic message when the body of elders laid their hands on you." [1 Timothy 4:14, emphasis mine].

The anointing is transferable through anointed audio-visual materials that come from a consecrated, God-fearing and anointed vessel of God! Examples include Moses' rod, Elijah's mantle, Elisha's mantle, Jesus' garment, the Apostle Paul's handkerchiefs and even his aprons. The Apostle Peter's shadow was so loaded with the anointing that it healed the sick on the streets!

Please hold on to this secret: The key to receiving the anointing is a burning desire –hunger, thirst and brokenness for the indwelling presence of the Holy Spirit and for the rain! Now that you have the secret don't delay! Go for it!

Let Your Faith Be Productive

FAITH IS LIKE A farmland where destinies are cultivated. Just like the farmer will always be found working on his farm weeding and tending to his crops, you must engage yourself in the productive working of your faith. Bishop David Oyedepo says, *"Faith is a profession not a confession."* A farmer working on his farm is supernaturally calling forth his harvest and in the fullness of time, his barn is full of his increase. In the same way, your miracles will manifest when you WORK your faith. Therefore, match your faith with outstanding actions and you will amass outstanding results to the glory of God the Father. As it is written:

"Show me your faith without your works, and I will show you my faith by my works." [James 2:18 NKJV].

Faith is tangible! The tangibility of your faith is evident in the work you are doing in accordance with that faith. Your faith must be visible! The clarity and maturity of your work are good descriptors of your faith. In other words; little works are pointers to little faith; great works are divine exhibitions of great faith at work. Dr Paul Enenche says; *"Do big things."* This implies: increase your imagination. Your faith grows not only with your Word level, but with your imaginative power. Why? Because your imagination determines your manifestation! You cannot do beyond what you can imagine. But today, the power of God is made available to you even in this book to receive the unction to imagine and to accomplish great things in Jesus' name.

"Now faith is the substance of things hoped for, the evidence of things not seen." [Hebrews 11:1 NKJV].

Let your faith produce evidence! Be so filled with hope in Christ that you begin to see only possibilities. It is your hope in Jesus alone that produces faith. When you are fully saturated with the word of God, you will begin to bring forth faith as children. Faith, when birthed is manifested and demonstrated by the actions you take, the boldness in your decisions, the skillfulness of your planning, the integration and articulation of your knowledge and finally, the divine execution of your heavenly vision. If you do not execute then you cannot take delivery! Execution of divine vision is your highway to a glorious destiny! Execute your God-given vision and receive a higher unction for a higher mandate! Work your faith, today! There is no faith without works because **"…Faith by itself, if it does not have works, is dead."** [James 2:17 NKJV].

Say this prayer: I receive grace now to walk my way to greatness as I activate and work my faith into productivity, in Jesus' name. Amen!

9
God Will Never Abandon You

JESUS SAYS: "AND SURELY I am with you always, to the very end of the age." [Matthew 28:20].

Sometimes betrayal serves as the catalyst you need to launch you into your destiny. Until Jesus was betrayed, He was not glorified. And after He was betrayed, abandoned and crucified, He became the "talk of the town", the sought after One, the Savior of the world, the LORD of lords, the King of kings, the Alpha and Omega, God Almighty. Don't hate those who have betrayed or abandoned you, but love them, because they are instrumental to announcing your greatness. Indeed, they are important motivators as you climb to the mountain top, and as such, you need them. The Psalmist said:

"You prepare a table before me in the presence of my enemies; you anoint my head with oil; my cup overflows. Surely goodness and love will follow me all the days of my life, and I will dwell in the house of the LORD forever." [Psalm 23:5, 6].

Your enemies add spice to your table, because great anointing and blessings are always released in the face of trials. James 1:2 says:

"My brethren count it all joy when you fall into various trials, knowing that the testing of your faith produces patience. But let patience have its perfect work, that you may be perfect and complete, lacking nothing."

You lack nothing when you weather the storms of life (including betrayals and rejection) through His grace, because your spirit man becomes all fired up through your trial. Your obedience in the face of suffering establishes you,, thus producing the blessings and rewards of obedience [see Deuteronomy 28:1-14] . Bishop Abioye says: *"The tougher your situation is the more guaranteed your victory."* To that I would add ,"The tougher your today, the more glorious your tomorrow!" Enemies and trials add spice to your life. When God displayed His mighty power against Pharaoh to deliver the Israelites, other nations heard about it and were paralyzed with the fear of God's people. As it is written:

"This very day, I will begin to put the terror and fear of you on all the nations under heaven. They will hear reports of you and will tremble and be in anguish because of you." [Deuteronomy 2:25].

Godly fear of you will disarm your enemies. May you receive the grace and wisdom to see beyond your sufferings and embrace by faith your victory. **"For everyone born of God overcomes the world. This is the victory that has overcome the world, even our faith."** [1 John 5:4].

10
Hold On To Your Promise

THOSE WHO GIVE UP don't go up! If you do not hold on, then you cannot go on! Hang in there to move into your Canaan! The Israelites were bruised in slavery in Egypt, but they held on to their promise!

"During that long period, the king of Egypt died. The Israelites groaned in their slavery and cried out, and their cry went up to God. God heard their groaning and He remembered his covenant with Abraham, with Isaac and with Jacob. So God looked on the Israelites and was concerned about them." [Exodus 2:23-25].

You too, are an heir of this same covenant. As the word says, "If you belong to Christ, then you are Abraham's seed, and heirs according to the promise." [Galatians 3:29];

"Now you, brothers, like Isaac are children of promise." [Galatians 4:28].

God is compelled by His word and covenant to establish your destiny gloriously if you believe in Him and walk in the understanding of this light. God says:

"But My righteous one will live by faith. And if he shrinks back, I will not be pleased with him." [Hebrews 10:38]

Friend, do not allow your faith to shrink back, because if God is not pleased with you, you certainly do not have His backing. Without God's backing, you cannot withstand your opposition. As the Scripture says; **"If God is for us who can be against us?"** [Romans 8:31] But, what if He is not with us? Then, everything and everyone will be against us! May heaven not permit that your faith shrinks in Jesus' name. Amen! May God sustain your faith from failing. Stand firm in the LORD and He will keep you from every shame! The truth is that every overcomer is entitled to a crown. Those who give up are already disqualified, But those who keep their heads from the deceits of the devil, who say **"If I perish, I perish…"**, [Esther 4:16] that fight and win, their crowns are guaranteed. Jesus said:

"I am coming soon. Hold on to what you have, so that no-one will take your crown. Him who overcomes I will make a pillar in the temple of my God. Never again will he leave it…Be faithful, even to the point of death, and I will give you the crown of life…He who overcomes will not be hurt at all by the second death…To him who overcomes, I will give some of the hidden manna. I will also give him a white stone with a new a name written on it, known only to him who receives it…Only hold on to what you have until I come…To him who overcomes and does My will to the end, I will give authority over nations…He who overcomes will, like them, be dressed in white. I will never blot out his name from the book of life, but will acknowledge his name before my Father and his angels….To him who overcomes, I will give the right to sit with me on my throne, just as I overcame and sat down with My Father on his throne. He who has an ear, let him hear what the Spirit says to the churches." [Revelation 3:11-12; 2:10-11, 17, 25-26; 3:5; 4:21].

In these scriptures, Jesus listed not only the rewards of those who did not give up but also made it so distinctively clear that it is our responsibility to overcome. In other words, Jesus implied that we have been endued with the power to overcome [Luke 10:19]. We no longer have the image of the first failed Adam. Instead, we have been recreated in the image, power and glory of the victorious Overcomer, the Lion of Judah, who is the last Adam, Jesus. He has handed over to us the same wisdom, strength, might and counsel which He employed to overcome his enemies [Matthew 13:11]. He empowers us to overcome just like He did.

Recognize your heavenly citizenship; you have a superior heritage; you were born not of this world but of and from heaven; you are not only natural, but spiritual [John 3:6], and you are from above and above all [1 Corinthians 15:44-54; Ephesians 2:6]. Those unbelievers whose citizenship is only from the earth fight and lose because they fight carnally. But not so with you! You triumph victoriously not just as a conqueror but more than a conqueror! Why? Because Jesus has redeemed you. His victory over the devil has become yours too! Walk in this knowledge of who you are, and open your mouth wide against the devil. God will fill your mouth with laughter as you see your enemies defeated. Hallelujah!

"What I am saying is that as long as the heir is a child, he is no different from a slave, although he owns the whole estate. He is subject to guardians and trustees until the time set by his father." [Galatians 4:1].

Regarding your covenant benefits, do not be a child anymore. Know who you are and mature in the knowledge of your redemptive inheritance! Do not let your faith shrink! If you don't give up on who you are, the devil will be forced to give up on you! Overcome, and do not shrink back. Don't shiver and quiver in fear, but be determined to dare and succeed. Set your face and heart like a flint of iron against the devil and his tricks. Don't give up, rather go up in faith, speech, action, and the fear of God. Stand tall, and be strong! Fight, conquer and celebrate your victory in Jesus' name! Amen.

11

Know When to Move Up

"THE LORD OUR GOD said to us at Horeb, "You have stayed long enough at this mountain. Break camp, and advance...." [Deuteronomy 1:6].

Advancement in life and ministry come when you recognize that you are stagnated and are overdue for a promotion. Rehearsing and relaxing over past achievements without moving forward has the potential of retarding your God-ordained promotion. Continue to rejoice, celebrate and testify as a lifestyle but move on to your next achievement because:

"From the days of John the Baptist until now the kingdom of heaven suffers violence, and the violent take it by force." [Matthew 11:12 NKJV].

If you have taken delivery of past successes and victories, don't stop, but continue to fight and win. Keep succeeding, and don't slumber or sleep because:

"While men slept his enemy came and sowed tares among the wheat and went his way. But when the grain had sprouted and produced a crop, then the tares also appeared." [Matthew 13:25, 26 NKJV].

Know When to Move Up

Your enemy, the devil, is not happy when you succeed. He will come at you with a spirit of complacency to make you lukewarm, and relaxed. He may tempt you with dangerous feelings of achievement, accomplishment or convince you that you have "arrived." Please say NO to all his tricks and fight on, remembering that:

"For though we walk in the flesh, we do not war according to the flesh. For the weapons of our warfare are not carnal but mighty in God for pulling down strongholds, casting down arguments and every high thing that exalts itself against the knowledge of God, bringing every thought into captivity to the obedience of Christ." [2 Corinthians 10:3-6 NKJV];

"For we wrestle not against flesh and blood, but against principalities, against powers, against the rulers of the darkness of this world, against spiritual wickedness in high places." [Ephesians 6:12 KJV].

The Apostle Paul said:

"Not that I have already obtained all this, or have already been made perfect, but I press on to take hold of that for which Christ Jesus took hold of me. Brothers, I do not consider myself yet to have taken hold of it. But one thing I do: *Forgetting what is behind* and straining toward what is ahead, *I press on* towards the goal to win the prize for which God has called me heavenwards in Christ Jesus." [Philippians 3:12-14, emphasis mine].

Friend, if after his great and eternal accomplishments, the Apostle Paul said, "...I press on...", then it is obvious that the road to continued success is called: "Keep pressing on" toward the kingdom of our great God until the day of the LORD. Beloved, it is wise to understand that wicked powers do not come armed with fiery revolvers; rather they come subtly, enticing people with laziness, compromises of Christ's standards, complacency, pride and arrogance! I thank God, however, because I know you understand and won't be fooled by the devil's devices. Keep your spiritual fire and fervor burning! Do great things for God! It is not over until the day the LORD himself returns!

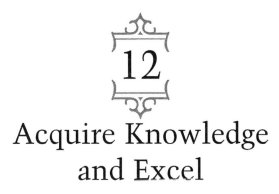

Acquire Knowledge and Excel

I DEFINE KNOWLEDGE, AS "knowing enough to have an edge over ignorance". Knowledge is your edge and will always work to your advantage.

"For this reason, since the day we heard about you, we have not stopped praying for you and asking God to fill you with the knowledge of his will through all spiritual wisdom and understanding." [Colossians 1:9].

The Apostle Paul understood that without knowledge the Colossians had no understanding of who they were and what they had in Christ. Because o f this, he labored in prayer for them, asking God to steer them towards a relationship, filled with the knowledge of him. What we see in church today are "fun lovers" and not believers who seek to know the Truth… This, as you know is very dangerous, for it is written:

"My people are destroyed for lack of knowledge; Because thou hast rejected knowledge, I will also reject thee, thou shalt be no priest to Me:

seeing thou hast forgotten the law of thy God, I will also forget thy children." [Hosea 4:6].

World-changers are those who labor in the word of God. That wise man, Daniel, said **"I, Daniel, understood from the Scriptures, according to the word of the LORD...."** [Daniel 9:2]. Understanding is a product of focused and disciplined labor in the word. Among his contemporaries, no one was found to be smarter than Daniel Concerning him it was written:

"There is a man in your kingdom who has the spirit of the holy gods in him. In the time of your father he was found to have insight and intelligence and wisdom like that of the gods." [Daniel 5:11].

Daniel said the Source of his wisdom was the "word" [Daniel 9:2]. To participate in this blessed walk with God, be sold out to the word of God. Do not just memorize scriptures but seek to know God and His perfect will for your life. Then you can walk before Him blameless in His sight. When you know the word, you know God, and when you truly know God then your fruitfulness, will be seen by all men. **"The people who know their God shall be strong, and carry out *great exploits.*"** [Daniel 11:32].

13
Let God Make You What You Ought to Be

AT ONE POINT IN my life, I wanted to be a medical doctor, and I saw myself in Zoology. I reasoned that "I'd become a diplomat through Zoology." I studied foreign languages for this purpose. In the process, I discovered that a first degree in Zoology would not be enough even with foreign languages so I enrolled into advanced degree. During this time, God was probably watching me, saying; *"After you're done with all these degrees, I will still make you My servant!"* Beloved, let God make you what He wants you to be. When you discover His purpose for your life it will will be free of struggles and full of testimonies! When Jesus beckoned to Simon Peter and his brother Andrew; **"'Come, follow me…and I will make you fishers of men.' At once they left their nets and followed Him,"** [Mark 1:17], they didn't quite understand the details, demands, and glory of their calling, but they willingly followed Him.

Jesus made a wonder out of unschooled local fishermen! Wherever Jesus is preached today, the names of these formerly "nothing-nobody-nowhere" fishermen are mentioned. As a result of their obedience to Jesus' call, He has made them pillars of the Gospel, and their names have been immortalized! Has Jesus stopped making wonders out "nobodies" like Peter and the disciples today? No! If you answer His call today, you too, will become a wonder to your generation.

I personally know a man who has stepped into this great grace: from insecurity to security; from an obscure future to a unique destiny, from confusion to celebration! Allow Christ to make you what He designed you to be. Follow and be a fool for Him and He will make you the wisest of all! Jesus told the rich young ruler:

"If you want to be perfect, go, sell your possessions and give to the poor; and you will have treasure in heaven. Then come follow me." [Matthew 19:21].

This young man declined Jesus' offer, and that was the last time the world has ever heard of him! Don't let your life end in obscurity; leave an eternal mark for God's glory. Jesus said:

"I tell you the truth…no one who has left home or brothers or sisters or mother or father or children or fields for me and the gospel will fail to receive a hundred times as much in this present age (homes, brothers, sisters, mothers, children and fields—and with them, persecutions) and in the age to come, eternal life." [Mark 10:29, 30].

To follow Jesus, you have to "sell" some of your "possessions"! You may have to give up your ambition, pride, friends, unholy relationships, greed, unforgiveness, unbelief, or some other thing. You have to let go of the flesh to take hold of the Spirit! But when you give up anything to follow Jesus, He says a heavenly account will be opened for you with benefits that no earthly financial house can match! The wisest investment anyone can make in life is to follow Jesus. He gives you eternal life and 100% of your initial investment! [see Mark 10:29, 30 above].

Sow Seeds of Unconditional Love

"BE VERY CAREFUL, THEN how you live—not as unwise but as wise, making the most of every opportunity, because the days are evil." [Ephesians 5:15].

You are on your way to greatness when you take the opportunity to sow seeds of love in someone's life. As you recognize these opportunities, you will be motivated to make the most of them and to continue to sow, whether it appears to be appreciated or not. The word says:

"Whoever sows sparingly will also reap sparingly, and whoever sows generously will also reap generously." [2 Corinthians 9:6].

Above all, show love to all as a conscious spiritual act of seed sowing. It is very powerful to see it that way and to expect rewards from God because "As long as the earth endures, seedtime and harvest…will never cease." [Genesis 8:22]. What's more, the more seed of love you sow the more harvest of all things you will have! Love is an imperishable, incorruptible seed that always produces a harvest of righteousness. Sow abundantly and you'll reap an abundant harvest of every good thing. At times it may be difficult to keep sowing love when your heart had been bruised, but never you mind, continue sowing generously. Hebrews 6:10 says:

"God is not unjust that; he will not forget your work and the love you have shown Him as you have helped his people and continue to help them."

When you show love to anyone, you are also sowing that seed of love into God's heart and God says He will reward you [Numbers 23:19-20]. Don't concern yourself about the reward from the people to whom you have shown love. Continue to love them and be assured that God will return that love to you in ways you have never expected, and watch as your life becomes more rewarding and meaningful than you ever imagined!

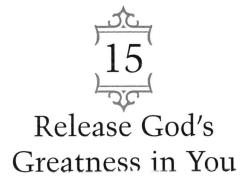

15

Release God's Greatness in You

"AGAIN THE ISRAELITES DID evil in the eyes of the LORD, and for seven years he gave them into the hands of the Midianites. Because the power of the Midian was so oppressive, the Israelites prepared shelters for themselves in mountain clefts, caves and strongholds. Whenever the Israelites planted their crops, the Midianites, Amalekites and other eastern peoples invaded the country." [Judges 6:1-3].

The Israelites were almost forced to live on top of mountains and underground because of the oppressive power of the Midianites. They were convinced that there was no one to deliver them and that they could not face their adversaries. So they cried out to God for a deliverer, even though there was one already among them! Gideon himself, who had the power of God to deliver his people, was paralyzed with fear. That is, until he had an encounter with God!

"The angel of the LORD came and sat down under the oak in Ophrah that belonged to Joash the Abiezrite, where his son Gideon was threshing wheat in a winepress to keep it from the Midianites. When the angel of the appeared to Gideon, he said, 'The LORD is with you, mighty warrior.'" [Judges 6:11, 12].

Gideon had no idea that he was God's warrior let alone a mighty one! Just like Gideon, you too are stronger than you realize! Israel was so paralyzed with fear, that it didn't recognize that God's deliverer was already among them! The same is true for you. Your deliverer, Jesus, is inside of you. Awake the sleeping lion within and you'll climb impossible mountains! When you realize that the greater One lives inside you, you'll accomplish great feats that will shock you! Don't worry about failing; be afraid not to try! You are the hope of this generation! Arise for your family, your church, your nation and your destiny. Otherwise, the spiritual, financial, material and physical oppression might continue. Quit hiding from opportunities in your family, church and workplace to be God's deliverer. Rise up to the challenge and let what's in you come out!

There is Someone greater and mightier than Gideon in you! It is Jesus in you! He is the Deliverer, He is the Solution and the Truth that will set you and the world around you free. Release Him from inside you by letting your faith work. You have been put here at this time to bring about change for this generation! Inside of you lies a sleeping lion! Jesus is in you and with Him you can accomplish anything! Wake up to who lives inside of you. Believe in Him, believe He can do it in you, believe He is great. Believe that Jesus in you can cause that long-awaited revival. Believe that with Him in you, you can pray down the fire. Believe that with Him in you, you can heal the sick , raise the dead and brutalize demons. Believe you can succeed, believe you can overcome, believe you can win! And above all, let Him do *it* in you NOW!

16

Make Your Move and Trust God to Perfect It

THE PERFECT MOMENT WAITS for those who do not wait for it. As Dr. Paul Enenche would say, *"Do it now!"* The Bible says:

"**Whatever you do, work at it with all your heart, as working for the LORD, not for men, since you know that you will receive an inheritance from THE LORD as a reward. It is the LORD Christ you are serving.**" [Colossians 3:23, 24].

This scripture says; "**Whatever you do…,**" not *whatever you do not do* and it says, "**work at it will all your heart,**" and not *"wait at it with all your time.".* As you enthusiastically work at your God-given vision, God will teach you the secrets of your commission and open up your understanding. Your obedience to and diligence for God will make His intelligence available to you! As you keep working diligently without waiting for that "perfect time" God will perfect your imperfections. As it is written:

"**…When perfection comes, the imperfect disappears.**" [1 Corinthians 13:10].

Jesus said:

"As long as it is day, we must do the work of him who sent me. Night is coming, when no one can work." [John 9:4].

Friend now is your *day*, do the work God has called you to now, and you'll be done before the night comes! People don't "work" at night **"For those who sleep, sleep at night…"** [1 Thessalonians 5:7] **"But since we belong to the day…"** [1 Thessalonians 5:8], and **"We do not belong to the night or to the darkness."** [1 Thessalonians 5:5] **"Let us not be like others, who are asleep, but let us be alert and self-controlled."** [1 Thessalonians 5:6]. Having received an inspiration from the Father, don't delay its execution. Rather, work towards its manifestation with all your might! Work at it now while it is still day.

17

Team Up with A Faithful God

REST IN GOD AND be encouraged! 1 Thessalonians 5:24 says **"The one who calls you is faithful and he will do it."** We hear often that we are *"doing the work of God."* From the human or natural point of view, yes, if indeed, we are doing it, if we are committed to our commission. But spiritually speaking, God is the One doing all the work!

"For it is God who works in you to will and to act according to his good purpose." [Philippians 2:13].

Just like the pot has no influence over the potter, we have no "say" (this is true for a believer that is totally yielded to the Holy Spirit)! As it is written; "But who are you, O man, to talk back to God? Shall what is formed say to him who formed it, 'Why did you make me like this?' Does not the potter have the right to make out of the same lump of clay some pottery for noble purposes and some for common use?" [Romans 9:20].

When God calls us into His service, He does it so that He may be glorified through us and in us. The colt upon which Jesus sat and rode was the only colt privileged to be used for such an honor. In the same way, we should see ourselves as privileged in our generation to be called of the LORD and to bear His name! But even though He has called us to perform a particular task, it is really Him doing the work through us. As the Scripture says:

"For it is God who works in you to will and to act according to his good purpose." [Philippians 2:13].

Jesus said:

"Don't you believe that I am in the Father, and that the Father in me? The words I say to you are not just my own. Rather, it is the Father, living in me, who is doing his work." [John 14:10].

Since it is God that actually does His work through us, let us then not be so heavily dependant on "supporters." Let's apply ourselves intensively to His mandate and then we will truly realize that, **"The one who calls you is faithful and he will do it."** [1 Thessalonians 5:24].

18

Purity Releases Power

THE FIRST STEP TO living a pure life is separation. This does not imply running away from family and friends or your local church, but rather separating your heart unto God alone who is able to keep you clean until the day of the Lord.

"Therefore come out from them and be separate…. Touch no unclean thing, and I will receive you. I will be a Father to you, and you will be my sons and daughters, says the LORD Almighty." [2 Corinthians 6:17-18] and as the Scripture says, "Rend your heart and not your garments. Return to the LORD your God, for He is gracious and compassionate." [Joel 2:13].

The second step is to separate yourself from the unclean lifestyle of the world. As it is written, "Do not conform any longer to the pattern of this world, but be transformed by the renewing of your mind." [Romans 12:2]. The kingdom of God and this world are two separate kingdoms. Our heavenly Father is in charge of His kingdom, while the devil controls this world. Jesus said:

"If the world hates you, keep in mind that it hated me first. If you belonged to the world, it would love you as its own. As it is, you do not belong to the world, but I have chosen you out of the world. That is why the world hates you." [John 15:18-19].

Jesus made a vivid distinction between this world and where He came from—God's kingdom, which is where He has also called us. 2 Corinthians 4:4 says, "**The god of this age [*world*] has blinded the minds of the unbelievers, so that they cannot see the light of the gospel of the glory of Christ, who is the image of God**" [*Emphasis mine*]. As clearly demonstrated by these scriptures (John 15:18, and 2 Corinthians 4:4), believers in Christ are not of this world (even though we are in it). Therefore, as a believer, living your life according to the pattern of this world robs you of your heavenly entitlements and benefits which include the demonstration of your divinity—the power of God. Jesus says, "**I have chosen you out of the world.**" [John 15:19] meaning you are called to be pure, not to be like the world but like Jesus. You have been **chosen!** You were separated and **called out** to be glorified...

"And those he predestined, he also called; those he called, He also justified; those he justified, He also glorified." [Romans 8:30].

"For God did not call us to be impure, but to live a holy life. Therefore, he who rejects this instruction does not reject man but God, who gives you His Holy Spirit." [1 Thessalonians 4:7, 8].

So, be conscious of your heavenly citizenship ("**Our citizenship is in heaven.**" [Philippians 3:20). And do not let what is passing away rob you of your eternal glory "For this world in its present form is passing away." [1 Corinthians 7:31]. Many great and glorious destinies have been derailed because they conformed to the deceptions of an eroding world.

"Do not conform any longer to the pattern of this world, but be transformed by the renewing of your mind. Then you will be able to test and approve what God's will is—His good, pleasing and perfect will." [Romans 12:2].

Now, the question for us is, "What is God's will?"

"It is God's will that you should be sanctified: that you should avoid sexual immorality; that each of you should learn to control his own body in a way that is holy and honorable, not in passionate lust like the heathen, who do not know God," [1 Thessalonians 4:3-5].

Concerning this matter then, let's take advice from 1 John 2:15 [NKJV] which says:

"Do not love the world or the things in the world. If anyone loves the world, the love of the Father is not in him. For all that is *in* the world—the lust of the flesh, the lust of the eyes, and the pride of life—is not of the Father but is of the world. And the world is passing away, and the lust of it; but he who does the will of God abides forever."

19

Trust God with Your Heart

"LET US FIX OUR eyes on Jesus, the author and perfecter of our faith." [Hebrews 12:2].

"Fix your thoughts on Jesus, the Apostle and High Priest whom we confess." [Hebrews 3:1].

The word "fix" is common to these two scriptures. It has several definitions, one of which means the *permanent* installation of a smaller object onto a larger one. For instance, you can fix a door bell onto your door frame. It also means "to have your attention focused on somebody or something." In the scriptures above, it means to depend totally and unshakably on Christ; trusting firmly and unrepentantly on Him who is able to deliver you and make you what you ought to be! This is very different from trusting in man, which the Father warned us not to do. Jeremiah shows us how very dangerous this can be:

"Curse is the one who trusts in man, who depends on flesh for his strength and whose heart turns away from the LORD. He will be like a bush in the wastelands; he will not see prosperity when it comes. He will dwell in the parched places of the desert, in a salt land where no-one lives. But blessed is the man who trusts in the LORD, whose confidence is in him. He will be like a tree planted by the water that sends out its roots by the stream. It does not fear when heat comes; its leaves are always green. It has no worries in a year of drought and never fails to bear fruit". [Jeremiah 17:5-8].

And here we see this reiterated:

"Do not trust a neighbour; put no confidence in a friend. Even with her who lies in your embrace, be careful of your words." [Micah 7:5].

Please do not misunderstand what these scriptures are saying. We all know that for any relationship to thrive, there has to be a reasonable degree of trust between the individuals involved. However, the confidence, dependence and trust we should have in God alone, should never be transferred to another individual or thing. Otherwise, you have made that person or thing you are trusting in your god, and that is the abominable sin of idolatry. Why we can totally trust in God is clearly laid out in Numbers 23:19:

"God is not a man that he should lie, nor a son of man, that he should change his mind."

Even if a man does not lie, he could possibly change his mind. And any man that speaks the truth and keeps his word no matter what the cost is to him is a man worthy of being associated with. I'd like to meet such a man! If Jesus had depended on His disciples when He was arrested, assaulted and crucified, he would not be our Savior today! He did not trust in man, but rather depended on his Heavenly Father who never abandoned him. .Here we see Jesus being betrayed by one of His disciples:

"While he was still speaking, Judas, one of the Twelve, arrived. With him was a large crowd armed with swords and clubs, sent from the chief priests and the elders of the people. Now the betrayer had arranged a signal with them: The one I kiss is the man; arrest him." [Matthew 26:47, 48].

And what about the rest of His disciples?

"Then all the disciples deserted Him and fled." [Matthew 26:56].

Even his closest friend:

"But Peter followed him at a distance, right up to the courtyard of the high priest…Then he (*Peter*) began to call down curses on himself and he swore to them, 'I don't know the man!' Immediately a rooster crowed. Then Peter remembered the word Jesus had spoken: 'Before the rooster crows, you will disown me three times." [Matthew 26:58, 74-75, emphasis mine].

You are profoundly wise, to commit into God's hands, the hearts of the people you come in contact with because **"The king's heart is in the hand of the LORD, like the rivers of water; He turns it wherever He wishes."** [Proverbs 21:1 NKJV]. God knows every heart. As it is written: **"But the LORD weighs the hearts."** [Proverbs 21:2 NKJV] As you commit all men you deal with to him, be assured that he will save you from the wicked and the deceivers. Jeremiah 17:9 asks, **"The heart is deceitful above all things, and desperately wicked; who can know it?** But the LORD himself answered;

"I, the LORD, search the heart, I test the mind, even to give every man according to his ways, according to the fruit of his doings." [Jeremiah 10:10].

Your heart is safer with God than it will ever be with man! He is able to make you what you ought to be and keep the secrets you entrust to Him. Trust in Him, depend on Him and make Him your confidante and be assured your destiny will be glorious!

20

Be Diligent In Your Work

"DO YOU SEE A [*diligent*] man who excels in his work? He will stand before kings; he will not stand before unknown [*mere, obscure*] men." [Proverbs 22:29, emphasis mine].

Undivided dedication, undistracted loyalty, total commitment, overwhelming zeal and willingness should be invested in whatever you desire to accomplish. Great destinies are forged when diligence and skillfulness become the rule of the day. Jesus said:

"The poor you will always have with you, but you will not always have Me." [Matthew 25:11].

Has Jesus designated some to be poor and others to be rich? Let's see:

"For you know the grace of our LORD Jesus Christ, that though He was rich, yet for your sakes He became poor, so that you through his poverty might become rich." [2 Corinthians 8:9].

By his death, Jesus has made everyone who believes in him rich. They are not just a candidate for blessings but a blessing personified. As it says in scripture:

"He redeemed us in order that the blessing given to Abraham might come to the Gentiles through Christ Jesus, so that by faith we might receive the promise of the Spirit." [Galatians 3:14].

Jesus became poor so that *we might become rich*. He redeemed us from the curse of poverty so that the *blessing* of Abraham *might come to each of us!* Then why did Jesus say, *"You will always have the poor with you?"* Does he play favorites? No. He said it because some people will unconsciously decide not to take the path to greatness. Why? The reasons are the same as explained by Jesus himself in the parable of the sower [Matthew 13:1-23]. Some people hear the message of the kingdom, but the devil comes and takes it away. Some hear the word with joy but it takes no root in them and is not nourished to fruition. Others hear the word but allow worries and the deceitfulness of wealth to choke it and make it unfruitful in their lives, while some, those truly wealthy in Christ, hear and understand and the word produces a hundred, sixty and thirty fold return of what was sown. [Scripture paraphrased]

This scripture is a vivid exposition of poverty in that it shows us what can happen if we don't take the word and its pursuit seriously. Why? Because:

"The knowledge of the secrets of the kingdom has been given to you, but not them. Whoever has will be given more, and he will have an abundance. Whoever does not have, even what he has will be taken from him." [Matthew 13:11-13].

The secret of success in life is knowledge of God's word. God said this through the prophet Hosea:

"My people are destroyed for lack of knowledge: because you have rejected knowledge, I also will reject thee, thou shalt be no priest to Me: seeing thou hast forgotten the law of thy God, I will also forget thy children." [Hosea 4:6].

Be Diligent In Your Work

Spiritual and physical poverty are clear evidence of a lack of knowledge and of obedience to the Word. Many people's destinies are wasted because some of God's people are either too lazy or *"too busy"* to eat the word or slow to obey the word they heard or studied! Another reason for poverty is idleness or laziness in doing meaningful work with our minds and hands.

The road to greatness is paved with *hard work!*

"**All hard work brings a profit, but mere talk leads only to poverty.**" [Proverbs 14:23].

"**Laziness brings on deep sleep, and the shiftless man goes hungry.**" [Proverbs 19:15].

Some great destinies are buried in beds because too many people in the kingdom are sleeping. People who love to sleep or prefer sleep over work are either poverty-stricken or are sleeping their way to the land of poverty. It is written:

"**Do not love sleep or you will grow poor; stay awake and you will have food to spare.**" [Proverbs 20:13].

It is pleasurable, however, to sleep after a hard day's work as the Scripture says:

"**'The sleep of a laborer is sweet, whether he eats little or much.**" [Ecclesiastes 5:12]

But sleep resulting from idleness and laziness is a destroyer; "**One who is slack in his work is brother to one who destroys.**" [Proverbs 18:9]. Decide today to eat the word of life. Be diligent to study God's word, and engage your mind and hands in meaningful work. You will be surprised when God promotes you! Wake up! Gather the light of the word and let Jesus shine through you in this dark world!

Don't Let Your Past Dictate Your Future

REGARDLESS OF VERY OUTSTANDING kingdom exploits, the Apostle Paul said:

"Brothers, I do not consider myself yet to have taken hold of it. But one thing I do: *Forgetting what is behind* and straining toward what is ahead, *I press on toward* the goal to win the prize for which God has called me heavenward in Christ Jesus." [Philippians 3:13-14, emphasis mine].

Your best yesterday, is not your best today, and your best today will not be as good as your best tomorrow. Don't let yesterday's accomplishments be your only reference point! The Apostle Paul's life and ministry is a huge challenge to the church today, where we take a nap after winning one soul, and we quit helping at church because someone has "insulted" us. He founded churches which led to the salvation of billions of souls; and He lived, walked in and performed many, many miracles. And he accomplished all this while being persecuted, and in the face of death. In spite of these obstacles he was able to say:

"...I do not consider myself yet to have taken hold of it. But one thing I do: Forgetting what is behind and straining towards what is ahead, I press on toward the goal to win the prize for which God has called me heavenward in Christ Jesus." [Philippians 3:13-14]. And Isaiah 43:18, 19 says: "Forget the former things; do not dwell on the past. See, I am doing a new thing! Now it springs up; do you not perceive it?"

Rise up above your bad days and years and overcome your frustrations and failures. Remember what God says:

"I will repay you for the years the locusts have eaten—the great locust and the young locust, the other locusts and the locust swarm—my great army that I sent among you. You will have plenty to eat, until you are full, and you will praise the name of the LORD your God who has worked wonders for you; never again will my people be shamed. [Joel 2:25-26].

Thank God for delivering you from all of yesterday's negative experiences! Testify to the goodness of God as you recall your accomplishments through His grace. And never think that the best you could ever be has already been accomplished.

Don't allow your destiny be retarded by your own success! Climb to greater heights! There is still so much more to be accomplished in the kingdom and in your life! Do more! Do "too much" in whatever you do!

You will have back in multiples anything you have lost in times past if you remain steadfast in Christ and put all your trust in Him! Your life is more than your bad times. They were just humbling experiences designed to bring you to the top! [Romans 8:28] Look beyond your frustrations and weaknesses and embrace your glorious destiny. As it is written:

"See, I am doing a new thing! Now it springs up; do you not perceive it?" [Isaiah 43:19]. "They only saw them and welcomed them from a distance [Hebrews 11:13].

See the new thing, **the new dawn of your new glory;** see *it*, believe *it*, embrace *it*; and become *it!*

22

Forgiveness: The Secret to An Open Heaven

"FOR IF YOU FORGIVE men when they sin against you, your heavenly Father will also forgive you. But if you do not forgive men their sins, your Father will not forgive your sins." [Matthew 6:14].

Where you will spend eternity should be every wise person's concern. Our eternal rest in heaven depends totally on us. No wonder the Apostle Paul wrote:

"**Continue to work out your salvation with fear and trembling.**" [Philippians 2:12].

Unforgiveness is one of Satan's subtle devices against God's saints to ensure they miss heaven! Why? Because if the devil cannot get you to commit the sin of sexual immorality, lies, greed, murder, slander etc. he will work through someone to offend you. And if you hold malice towards others and find it difficult to forgive offences, then you need to ask God for His grace to help you to forgive. The danger of unforgiveness is that you can't always see it on the surface because it is a matter of the heart. People can laugh, visit and even dance with their offenders and still gravely despise them. As the Scripture says:

"The heart is deceitful above all things and beyond cure. Who can understand it?" [Jeremiah 17:9].

The truth is that it takes the grace of God to truly forgive someone who has offended you. So, we need to ask God for the baptism of the grace to forgive. Whether unforgiveness is a two-way or one-way event, Jesus said:

"If you are offering your gift at the altar and there remember that your brother has something against you, leave your gift there in front of the altar. First go and be reconciled to your brother; then come and offer your gift." [Matthew 5:23].

People who are wise, humble, and who truly fear God should not find it difficult to own up their faults and apologize. Similarly, people who have been offended, should with love, make known their grievances to their offenders so that the matter can be resolved: As Jesus said:

"If your brother sins against you, go and show him his fault, just between the two of you. If he listens to you, you have won your brother over. But if he will not listen, take one or two others along, so that every matter may be established by the testimony of two or three witnesses.' If he refuses to listen to them, tell it to the church; and if he refuses to listen even to the church, treat him as you would a pagan or a tax collector." [Matthew 18:15-17].

How would you treat a pagan or a tax collector? Treat him with love! Jesus demonstrated this with Zacchaeus, the chief tax collector by having supper with him. Zacchaeus' heart melted at the kind of love Jesus showed him; he repented instantly and restored all he had looted from the people.

Forgiveness: The Secret to An Open Heaven

Jesus understood that Zacchaeus, a pagan, had no knowledge of salvation, which is God's love demonstrated through forgiveness of sins. Jesus considered Zacchaeus' soul of primary importance! Let us strive to imitate Jesus! Who knows, you might still save your brother's life from destruction! And please do not act like a pagan, because a man that cannot forgive sins nor repent for his faults acts just like one!

23
Read to Lead

PEOPLE WHO LACK WISDOM have nothing constructive to offer. To lead with excellence, embrace the godly habit of reading God-inspired literature. If you learn from the wise, you'll become wise yourself and you will inspire others. Solomon knew he couldn't lead without wisdom, so he asked God for it. His secrets have been revealed to us in the Word:

"He who walks with the wise grows wise, but a companion of fools suffers harm." [Proverbs 13:20].

Do you know that by reading a book from an anointed minister of Christ, you have become one of his friends? By gleaning from his books, tapes and videos, you're tapping into his wisdom which will rub off on you!! The truth is that you're not only partaking of his anointing but also from the wisdom he's gleaned from others. The reality is that by feeding your spirit with anointed materials your thinking, priorities, character and approach to life change for the better! In fact, your understanding will open up in a very practical way when you begin to walk with wise people even though you may never have met any of them in person! You become wise by studying anointed materials, how much more will you become wise by walking with those around you who are wise? Let their godly lives challenge you. Study their reverent submission to God; listen to the words of wisdom that they speak. Watch their prudent lifestyle, and let their godly example inspire you to a greater understanding in God!

And if by studying anointed books, tapes and videos and by walking with the wise around you, you gain wisdom, imagine how much more wise you'll become when you walk with Jesus, the wisdom of God Himself ["**...Christ the power of God and the wisdom of God.**" [1 Corinthians 1:24]]. Learn to walk with Jesus on daily basis. How? Jesus is a Person; the second Person in the Godhead. You can relate to Him in the same way you relate to a friend you see face to face. Set aside time to spend with Jesus. Praise Him, talk and listen to Him, worship Him. He wants to be your most intimate friend so that He can teach you His heart and His ways. As you do this you will become wise and your wisdom, which indeed is His, will impact generations until the day of our Jesus Christ!

24

Listening to God

"LISTEN, MY SON, TO your father's instruction and do not forsake your mother's teaching. They will be a garland to grace your head and a chain to adorn your neck." [Proverbs 1:8].

Your destiny is full of grace and glory when your ears are full of God's instructions and your feet are prompt to obey them! You will not suffer or experience shame or peril when you take instructions from the Master Himself and let Him lead you before you act. It is not only your willingness that counts, but your obedience as well. Isaiah 1:19 says:

"If you are willing and obedient, you will eat the best from the land."

You cannot obey what you do not hear, and you cannot hear if you do not listen. Develop a lifestyle of listening to God in all you do; then do whatever he says, and you will live in the realm of the miraculous. Here's an example of the benefits of listening:

"[Jesus'] mother said to the servants, 'Do whatever He tells you.... Jesus said to the servants, 'Fill the jars with water'; so they filled them to the brim. Then He told them, 'Now draw some out and take it to the master of the banquet.' They did so, and the master of the banquet tasted the water that been turned into wine." [John 2:5-9].

If you can hear Jesus' voice and do what He tells you, you can live in miracles everyday. Stop needlessly suffering and struggling, start enjoying life by heeding His voice. Then your obstacles will be turned into miracles!

25

A New Heart for a New Glory

THE OLD MAN MUST die for the new man to rise. The old cloth must be put off for the new dress to be worn. The body must receive a bath before a new dress is worn! A new heart for a new glory! A clean eye for sanctified insights! A clean imagination for a sacred destination! A sanctified thought for fresh oil!

"No one sews a new patch of unshrunk cloth on an old garment, for the patch will pull away from the garment, making the tear worse. Neither do men pour new wine (*the anointing*) into old wineskins. If they do, the skins will burst, the wine will run out and the wineskins will be ruined. No, they pour new wine into new wineskins, and both are preserved." [Matthew 9:16-17, emphasis mine].

It is a dangerous thing for God's power to fall on an unclean vessel. God wants to work through all His children to demonstrate the power of Jesus Christ so there will be a continual harvest of souls into His kingdom. But are we ready for the continuous flow of the raw power of God? The anointing of God is a consuming fire like in the days of Elijah. It has the ability to consume both the vessel and the sacrifice! I presume that God would rather not release His power than kill the very people He redeemed! No wonder Jesus said:

"Yet a time is coming and has now come when the true worshippers will worship the Father in spirit and truth, for they are the kind of worshippers the Father seeks. God is spirit, and His worshippers must worship in spirit and in truth." [John 4:23-24].

This is amazing! God is *seeking* those who will worship Him in spirit and truth, who have positioned their hearts for His anointing and the release of His raw power. Many want this power but only a few have it because they have gone the extra mile to sanctify and consecrate themselves for soul-winning through the power of the Holy Spirit! The truth is that a whole lot of believers are struggling with the flesh. Many really want to change so that they can bear fruit for Christ and not live in deception, but they keep falling. The Apostle Paul said:

"For what I want to do I do not do, but what I hate I do." [Romans 7:15].

The Scripture says; "Not by might nor by power, but by my Spirit." [Zechariah 4:6].

Although you cannot live a holy and pure life through your own effort, it all begins by recognizing that an impure heart is sinful and taking a bold step to end every deceptive lifestyle you are involved in. Since we cannot change ourselves, we must go to Him who has the power to take away our sin. By asking for His help He will give you the power and strength to overcome your weaknesses through His grace. Jesus Himself said:

"Come to me, all you who are weary and burdened, and I will give you rest." [Matthew 11:28].

Lay every impurity at His feet and ask Him to take the burden away from you and He will! It is only Jesus that can cleanse our bodies which are His temple. As the Apostle Paul wrote:

"Don't you know that you yourselves are God's temple and that God's Spirit lives in you? If anyone destroys God's temple, God will destroy him; for God's temple is sacred, and you are that temple." [1 Corinthians 4:16-17].

Jesus demonstrated how clean and undefiled His temple must be. He was outraged at the money changers' gross disrespect for the temple of God. In Mark 11:15-17 it reads:

"On reaching Jerusalem, Jesus entered the temple area and began driving out those who were buying and selling there. He overturned the tables of the money changers and benches of those selling doves, and would not allow anyone to carry merchandise through the temple courts. And as he taught them, he said, 'Is it not written: "My house will be called a house of prayer for all nations?"' [Mark 11:15-17].

If Jesus cleansed the man-made temple bearing His Name how much more the temple He made by himself for himself, your heart, and your body! Call upon him today and he will purify your heart. Then, he will release His raw power in you and his anointing will not consume you, but it will keep you blameless until the last day!

26

Believe and See

JESUS SAID:, "EVERYTHING IS possible for him that believes." [Mark 9:23].

This, you may say, sounds way too easy to be true! But God's word is truth (**"Your word is truth."** John 17:17). Your only possible limitation in life is *yourself!* Why? Because it is only you that can make you succeed or fail. God has given you everything you need. According to Bishop David Oyedepo: *"If you succeed, you did something to make it happen, and if you fail, you also did something to make it happen."* The truth is that everything is not possible for everyone; everything is possible for only those who *believe* that *"it is possible"*!

"As Jesus went on from there, two blind men followed him, calling out, 'Have mercy on us, Son of David!' When He had gone indoors, the blind men came to him, and he asked them, 'Do you *believe* that I am able to do this?' 'Yes,' they replied. Then He touched their eyes and said, 'According to your faith will it be done to you'; and their sight was restored." [Matthew 9:27-30, emphasis mine].

Jesus wanted these two blind men to understand that the restoration of their sight was in their own hands, and depended solely on whether they believed He could heal them or not! Having established that their faith was ready for a miracle, Jesus healed them! Their sight was not restored until their faith was in place. Your restoration, your prosperity, your joy, your peace, your success and your victory, is according to your faith, and is released upon you when you release your faith to receive them!

Beloved, your miracle is not according to your problems, family background, the national economy, the doctor's report, or your paycheck. It is not according to false accusations, your enemies' wishes, your education, experience, or your employers' decision, nor to anything or anyone in this wide world. It is only according to your faith, and whether you trust Jesus enough to believe that He is able to do what you need.

If you do trust Jesus, then look down at your troubles, take God's Word and give your problems their marching orders! Everything is possible for those who believe. Everything means *everything*; it includes anything you desire, or are faced with. You can get *it*, become *it*, achieve *it*, overcome *it* and there is absolutely *nothing* that can withstand you!

"What are you, O mighty mountain? Before Zerubbabel you will become level ground." [Zechariah 4:7].

It is impossible for you to be swallowed up in your *problem*; for that *mountain* to dwarf you; for that *dream* to drown you; for your *enemies* to have the last laugh; for the *world* not to hear about you. You are too much for failure and mediocrity. You have come way too far to retreat and you are too much for pity! You are not a byword! Nothing is impossible with and for you if you dare to believe that God who is with you and in you can do it. As for me, I do not see you failing, because I know that you are too loaded and too well placed (**"And God raised us up with Christ and seated us with him in the heavenly realms in Christ Jesus." [Ephesians 2:6]**) to fail!

27

Take the High Road in Jesus

OPTIMAL DEDICATION FOR OPTIMAL performance! Higher levels of focus for higher levels of achievement! Determination dries up your doubt; dedication destroys your distractions and your focus starves the devil to shame. When you are determined the demons are crippled and your will is established.

"**You will also declare a thing, and it will be established for you; so light will shine on your ways.**" [Job 22:28 NKJV].

If you say "yes" to God, He says "yes" to you, and your angels are discharged to carry out the heavenly order on your behalf. Until you arise nothing arises, until you arise no light shines [**Arise, shine for your light has come…** Isaiah 60:1]. Until you declare *it, it* will not be established, and until *it* is established no light shines! What are you waiting for? Rise up with determination and accomplish the unaccomplished! "**Arise, shine; for your light has come! And the glory of the L**ORD **is risen upon you.**" [Isaiah 60:1].

The only one that can hold you down is you! Quit losing inner energy, get the Word, open your mouth in prayer and demonstrate its power; for you have been called into the order of signs and wonders ["**Here am I and the children the Lord has given me! We are for signs and wonders.**" Isaiah 8:18]. Do not wait to be encouraged, rather encourage yourself in the Lord as David did: "**Now David was greatly distressed, for the people spoke of stoning him, because the soul of all the people was grieved, every man for his sons and daughters. But David *strengthened himself* in the Lord his God.**" [1 Samuel 30:6 NKJV, emphasis mine].

Something happened after David encouraged himself in the Lord: heaven released upon him strength, power and the anointing to overcome, to conquer and to accomplish. As it is written:

"**And He [*God*]) answered him [*David*], 'Pursue, for you shall surely overtake them and without fail recover all.'**" [1 Samuel 30:8, emphasis mine].

Be so determined that you may be able to mine your blessings from their Source. Be determined, focused, dedicated and highly self-motivated. Only a few people may encourage you and sometimes none will! Give attention to heaven through prayer and worship and heaven will give you attention! That's all you need! A heavenly backing! Friend, I say it again; be highly determined in your life and ministry. Success answers very readily to decision, determination, dedication and discipline! I believe you can make it, and I know that you too, know fully well that you can make it! Why? Because God says:

"**What you decide on will be done, and light will shine on your ways. When men are brought low and you say 'Lift them up!' then he will save the downcast.**" [Job 22:28-29]

Don't allow yourself to be downcast but instead, lift men up! When people see your focus and indefatigability they too, will be challenged and stirred onto greater exploits! You are a sign, a point of positive reference and an encouragement in the kingdom of God. It is time for people to begin to say; "If he can make it, I, too, can make it!

Please remember this: The world needs you to be able to succeed! You are the solution to their problems. Jesus says that you are both the light and the salt of the world. But if a solution becomes a problem himself, then the world is doomed and men are without hope! God forbid!

I'll say it again: Be highly determined. Your excellence and indeed, your uniqueness are clear reflections of your determination! Without determination men are tossed from one decision and vision to another without accomplishing anything. But not so with you, for I see you rising up now with a heart of decision, determination, dedication and discipline for higher level manifestation! From now on, pursue, overtake and recover all your plundered and delayed blessings. Enough is enough! Arise!

28

Don't Procrastinate

A MAN OF NOBLE character may lose his trust and value when he gambles with matters of great relevance. Opened doors of opportunities and success do not wait for the sluggards, the indecisive, the slothful and the "on-the-fence sitters"! Dr. Paul Enenche says: *"Delay brings decay!"* Many great destinies have totally decayed because someone was slothful, indecisive, "inattentative," procrastinated and was totally indifferent to challenges of great importance.

"Your servant went into the thick of the battle, and someone came to me with a captive and said 'Guard this man. If he is missing, it will be your life for his life, or you must pay a talent of silver.' While your servant was busy here and there, the man disappeared. 'That is your sentence,' the king said. 'You have pronounced it yourself.'" [1 Kings 20:39-40].

The man was *"busy here and there"* in a battlefield where swords, spears and arrows were flying all around, thus toying with his life and jeopardizing national security, peace and prosperity! The devil is throwing swords and arrows and spears and more deadly weapons around even more fiercely in our day [Ephesians 6:16], so much so, that we must not take our lives

Don't Procrastinate

for granted anymore. Destinies are in great danger when men gamble with issues of great importance. The man was *busy* doing the irrelevant, thus abandoning the urgently relevant challenges. That was starkly dangerous!

That is why it is of utmost importance to have a plan and to focus your attention on it religiously and with every amount of determination, passion and force you can muster. If you are busy doing *everything* you will end up doing *nothing*. If you are busy doing *nothing* you will end up doing *harm* to yourself. Do not procrastinate with what you can do now and put it off until next *time*, or the time after that. Severe damage has been done to many a destiny, marriage, relationship, business, finance, ministry and life because nothing was done. But if you're busy doing relevant things with undistracted diligence, greatness will become your endpoint.

Delay is cunning, crafty and deadly. The king said **"That is your sentence…you have pronounced it yourself."** Delay and procrastination are death sentences! A student that delays in studying cannot expect magic on the day of examination. Likewise, a man of God that seldom labors in the word or prays cannot expect a release of God's power and glory at the altar. What is more, a believer that hears the Word but delays to put it into practice is actually delaying the miraculous in his own life.

But you have encountered the power to change in Jesus' name! May you receive the grace now to do the important things proactively in Jesus' name!. May God release upon you the "Start-and-Finish" anointing. From today your hands will start and finish what you begin. You will receive the grace to attend to the important issues with speed and wisdom! May the wisdom and strength of God be released upon you to accomplish great things! May every spirit of indecision, hesitation and procrastination receive the judgment of God now! And may every decaying destiny be restored to you now, in Jesus' name. Amen!

Let God Teach You

HE SAYS; "CALL TO Me and I will answer you and tell you great and unsearchable things you do not know." [Jeremiah. 33:3].

In Proverbs 1:23 God says; **If you had responded to my rebuke, I would have poured out my heart to you and made my thoughts known to you."**

We are not acting smart when we step away from God. Life is a journey, and God has the roadmap and itinerary. He knows our schedules and our destinations. He knows which bus, train or flight will reach its destination successively. If we depend only on our own wisdom, we may miss our flight and end up on another man's destination.

"Come near to God and he will come near to you." [James 4:8].

If bad company corrupts good manners [1 Corinthians 15:33] and **"He who walks with the wise grows wise."** [Proverbs 13:20], then walking with God, and *"hanging out"* with Him will cause his glory to erupt from and distinguish you. If we reflect on the men who walked intimately with God, it may shed some light on our own spiritual journey:

"Enoch walked with God; then he was no more, because God took him away." [Genesis 5:24].

Enoch loved God so much and walked so intimately with Him that God may have said *"Enoch my friend will never see death nor decay."* May God say that about you and me! God preferred that Enoch come over to heaven *alive* so that both of them would always be together. The time has come for the Enochs of this day to be revealed.

What about Noah? At a time when sin and wickedness consumed creation to such a degree that God was grieved, Noah found favor with God! Genesis 6:6, 8-9 says:

"The LORD was grieved that He had made man on the earth, and His heart was filled with pain. So the LORD said, 'I will wipe mankind, whom I have created, from the face of the earth—men and animals, and creatures that move along the ground, and birds of the air—for I am grieved that I have made them. But Noah found favor in the eyes of the LORD.… Noah was a righteous man, blameless among the people of his time, and he walked with God."

You can just imagine what kind of sacred, intimate and exclusive relationship Noah had with God, that of all the men on earth, Noah was the only man that God favored. No wonder He chose him to replenish the earth! And there are more men like this: Abraham, Moses, Joshua, Samuel, David, and Elijah who was also taken to heaven alive. Elijah felt and shared the pains and visions of God. He was totally angered at the backsliding of Israel and he prayed so fervently that God made the rain cease from falling for $3\,^1/_2$ years! Do you feel what God feels? Are you satisfied with only going to church every Sunday and feel no pain in your heart when you see souls perish?

Are you much more interested in enriching yourself with the blessings of God than you are with enriching heaven with the souls he sent us to harvest [Mark 16:15-18]? It is well known that the son that is closest to his father will not only receive the father's wisdom but will also know the father's secrets of success, and ultimately receive the father's blessings. Esau was a man of the field, a game man, an outdoor man; but Jacob was an indoor man, not going far from his father. Jacob preferred to stay close to the source of his blessing than to look for the blessing away from the source!

Jacob was a kingdom-minded man, staying closest to the "king" of the kingdom, thus receiving the keys to the treasures of the kingdom! No wonder, when it was time for a change in kingship, there was no one qualified enough to take over except him. Why? Because Esau, the one who should have inherited the kingdom was never close enough to the King who is also the kingmaker! Are you a "God-man," a "world-man" or a "society-man"? Are you a "public-figure" or a "kingdom-figure"? Beloved, the closer you come to God the more He teaches you about Himself. Then he can trust you with kingdom secrets and treasure. As you allow him to tell you about your strengths and weakness, the more He will clean you up and get you ready for greater kingdom exploits. The more you learn about His ways, the brighter the glory of your star will become. As it says in 2 Corinthians 3:18:

> "But we all, with unveiled face, beholding as in a mirror the glory of the Lord, are being transformed into the *same* image from glory to glory, just as by the Spirit of the Lord." [2 Corinthians 3:18 NKJV]

When we behold Him from a distance, we cause ourselves to be far from understanding Him! But the closer we draw to Him, the better we understand Him! Until we come close to Him we may not close up the gaps in our lives! What else might we miss when we distance ourselves from Him? We may not know how wonderful He tastes! Psalm 34:8 says **"Taste and see that the LORD is good; blessed is the man who takes refuge in him."** No matter how wonderful a chef may cook, if no-one tastes his food his good work goes unappreciated. And no matter how much you want to taste his food, if you never visit his house or sit down at his table you will never have the opportunity to appreciate his cooking expertise! It is when you abide closely with God that you can smell His glory and indeed, partake of it!

Job was another man that walked so closely with God that he says of himself in the Word:

"Oh for the days when I was in my prime, when God's intimate friendship blessed my house." [Job 29:4].

Job had an intimate relationship with God; he knew God so much that even when he was afflicted beyond what any of us could bear he never cursed God, but rather said; **"Though He slay me, yet will I trust Him."** [Job 13:15 NKJV]. Friend, if you have an intimate relationship with God, you will have access to the deep secrets and treasures of His kingdom. If you only fish on the water's surface your nets will never be full until you launch into the deep. **"Deep calls to deep."** [Psalm 42:7]. A deep relationship with God will take you to the profound things of God. Every believer has access to God through the blood of Jesus, but not every believer has access to the deep things of God. His greatest riches are for those believers who long for and who have deep relationships with Him, because only a deep person in the Lord can call unto the deep treasures of our deep God! God Himself said:

"Call to me and I will answer you and tell you great and unsearchable things you do not know." [Jeremiah. 33:3].

30 THINGS I TELL MYSELF AND OTHERS

Like Job, you can walk very intimately with God and be distinguished in this world. Job, the Bible says:

"Was the *greatest* man among all the people of the East." [Job 1:3].

Job was not just great; he was the greatest man among all his people! And in Job 22:23-24, the secret of Job was exposed:

"If you return to the Almighty, you will be restored: If you remove wickedness far from your tent and assign your nuggets to the dust, your gold of Ophir to the rocks in the ravines, then the Almighty will be your gold, and the choicest of silver for you. Surely then you will find delight in the Almighty and will lift your face up to God. You will pray to Him, and He will hear you, and you will fulfill your vows."

Job says *"If you return to the Almighty!"* I see you returning *completely* to God today! You become a wonder to this generation. You do not have to cry for what belongs to your Father. Don't cry for your own inheritance! But if you do not know your Father well enough for Him to entrust the keys of His treasures to you, weeping may become inevitable! When God becomes your gold and choicest silver; when He becomes your very Treasure, your most important Possession, the One you need and the only "Thing" you ever desire, then He will make you wash your feet with butter and make gold the dust of your feet! All you need is your God, the Almighty God! Fall in love with Him very, very deeply! You know the way to your Father: Jesus is the Way. Be born again, if you are not: consume the word with passion; spend quality time alone with Him in prayer; worship Him extensively and intensively. Share your deepest secrets with Him and make Him your All. Walk in righteousness and purity of heart; give yourself to His church and His work; know the Holy Spirit and walk with Him and never leave the side of the Person of Jesus! Halleluiah!

30
Don't Repeat Your Failures.

GET A REVELATION FROM the Word for that overdue promotion in your life. Engage the ministry of the Holy Spirit and He will guide you to that truth which you need. When you find the truth (in the Word) and consciously engage with it, then your light will break forth. This is because it is only the truth that will set you free:

"Then you will know the truth, and the truth will set you free." [John 8:32].

Failure is a form of darkness which flourishes in ignorance, which they say is no excuse at all! Locate the keys to your treasure which Jesus already has released to the church. As He said:

"I will give you the keys of the kingdom of heaven." [Matthew 16:19]

And in Matthew 13:11 Jesus said; "The knowledge of the secrets of the kingdom of heaven has been given to you, but not to them."

When you get the knowledge, you have an edge over failure. Why? Because without knowledge, people perish. They fail; they suffer; they grope in darkness. They die like mere men when indeed they are not just human beings but the sons of God that have been sent to deliver man and to demonstrate divinity! Jesus already has given us the keys:

"I will give you the keys of the kingdom of heaven." [Matthew 16:19]

The keys are the secrets Jesus is referring to in Matthew 13:11. You cannot access any treasure, be it worldly or heavenly, without keys. Treasures are usually hidden, which is why they are called treasures in the first place! And, that's why Proverbs 25:2 says;

"It is the glory of God to conceal a matter; to search out a matter is the glory of kings."

In the same way you cannot pick a piece of gold or diamond from off the street, God said, you cannot just pick a revelation from the word by mere flipping through the pages but it is gained by searching; by conscious, deliberate and meticulous consultation of the word, and books, tapes, CDs, and DVDs of the forerunners of the kingdom ahead of you. It takes research! *What* you do not know, you will never know until you search it out and know *it for yourself;* and until you know *it*, it is your mountain, a dark alley and of course, a place of inevitable failure! But the day you make up your mind to search it out from the Word with the help of the Holy Spirit, your light will come. When your light comes, every form of darkness (failure, sickness, disease, disappointment, stagnation, frustration, barrenness, poverty, oppression, and sin) will disappear in a flash!

No matter how thick darkness may be, it succumbs very readily to the slightest glimmer of light. As the Scripture says:

"The light shines in the darkness, and darkness has not understood it." [John 1:5].

Darkness will never understand the power and revelation of the Word. It is not given to the prince of darkness (i.e. the devil) to understand

Don't Repeat Your Failures

how God and His Word work, rather he has to disappear when the light of the word of God is turned on in a believer's life! Let the Holy Spirit shine light on God's Word and watch as the forces of wickedness flee, As you continue to do so, you will walk victoriously all the days of your life! That is your revolution which guarantees your liberation which in turn gives birth to your celebration! Amen!

Acknowledgement:

I wish to acknowledge and thank the following ministers of the Gospel for their impact in my life and ministry: My beloved leader; Dr. (Pastor) Paul Enenche: Dunamis International Gospel Center, Abuja, Nigeria. Rev. P.I. Wisdom: Liberty Chapel International Churches, Lagos Nigeria. Rev. Israel Shadrach: Christian Pentecostal Mission, Abuja Nigeria. Bishop David Oyedepo: Faith Tabernacle, Ota, Ogun State, Nigeria. Bishop T.D. Jakes: Potter's House, Dallas Texas, USA., Pastor Sunday Adelaja: The Embassy of the Blessed Kingdom of God for All Nations, Kyiv Ukraine and Bishop David Ibeleme: Victorious Faith Ministries World Outreach, Belmont, Trinidad and Tobago. I thank Mr. and Mrs. Eze Onwuneme, my foster parents, who God has used to bless my life in so many unspeakable ways. I thank Grace, my beloved wife for always being my girl. Finally, I thank The Powermine family in Winnipeg and across the globe for their tremendous love and support.

About The Author

Pastor Ike Isinguzo is the Senior Pastor of The Powermine International, a Pentecostal church with its headquarters in Winnipeg Manitoba, Canada. He is married to Grace Isinguzo and the LORD blessed them recently with Nmesomachukwu and Ulomachukwu, their twin girls.